MW00885035

presentation :

This book was created for children, to be able to get them to start coloring and writing with the help of these very beautiful and themed drawings. The last part has been left blank with no drawings to stimulate the children's imagination.
I intend to continue to publish in this vein by changing gender.

emilcookie03@gmail.com

BUFFET

BUFFET

PIGTAILS

SKINNY

LITTLE GEISCHA

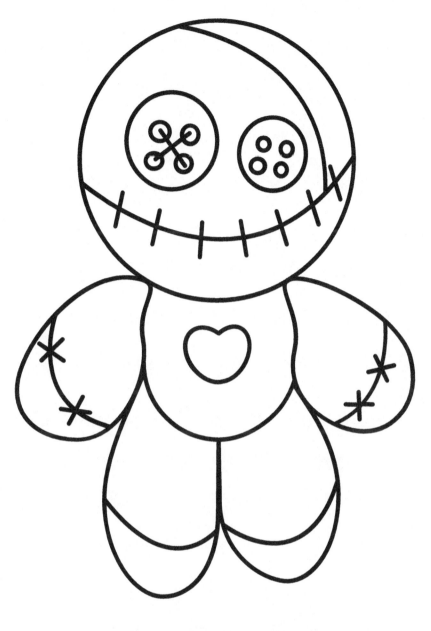

BUTTON

LITTLE ELF

LITTLE ELF

CARE BEAR

SLEEPY

SLEEPY

TEDDY BEARS

DOGGIE

DINOSAUR

NICE

UNICORN

SWAN PRINCESS

LITTLE DRESS

CAKE

CAKE

CUPCAKE

CANDIES

DIAMOND RING

NAILS

LIPSTICK

PERFUME BOTTLE

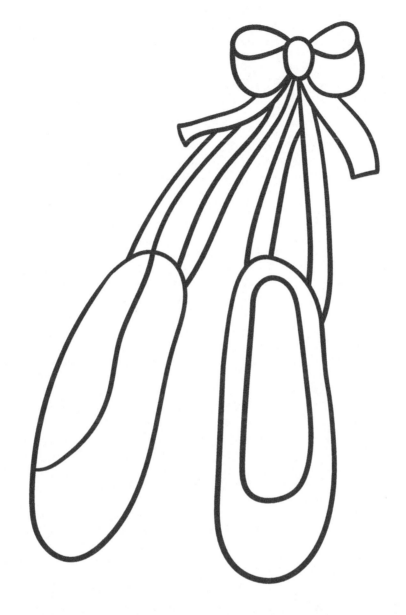

DANCING SHOES

FLOWERS

FLOWERS

CELL PHONE

- -

- -

SNOWMAN

VIDEO GAME COMMAND

MAGICAN

LITTLE BROTHERS

BALLON

ICE CREAM

TURKEY

TURKEY

FOX

SQUIRREL

SQUIRREL

REFRIGERATOR

WHIP

WHIP

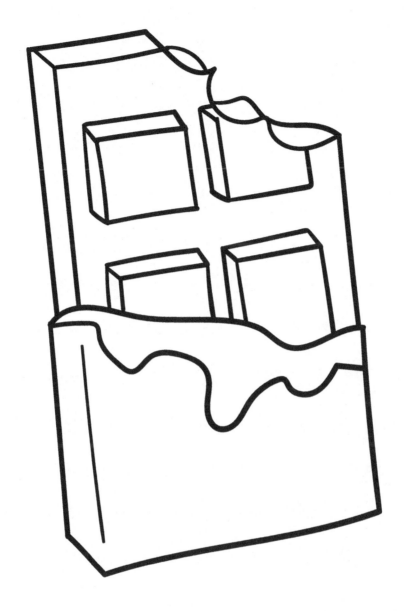

CHOCOLATE

CUP

WAKE UP

- -

- -

SLIPPERS

COMPUTER

COMPUTER

DOG

DOG

GIRL

GIRL

PORCUPINE

PORCUPINE

HAIRSTYLES

SMILE

BOY

COMIC STRIP

SALAD

- -

FRUIT

FRUIT

Made in the USA
Monee, IL
14 December 2024

73700612R00111